PAPER CAPERS

Jack Botermans

PAPER CAPERS

AN AMAZING ARRAY OF GAMES, PUZZLES, AND TRICKS

An Owl Book

HENRY HOLT AND COMPANY

New York

Copyright © 1986 by Plenary Publications International (Europe) bv, De Meern, The Netherlands
and ADM International bv, Amsterdam,
The Netherlands

Published in the United States by Henry Holt and
Company, Inc., 521 Fifth Avenue, New York,
New York 10175.

Published simultaneously in Canada.

Originally published in Holland under the
title *Spelen met Papier en Karton.*

Library of Congress Cataloging — in — Publication
Data.

Botermans, Jack.
Paper capers.

Translation of: Spelen met Papier en Karton.
'An Owl Book.'
1. Paper work. i. title
TT870.B65513 1986 745.54'86-7596

ISBN 0-8050-0139-5 (pbk.)

First American Edition

Text: Rob van den Dobbelsteen
Photography: David van Dijk
Models: Jeannet Leendertse

Printed in The Netherlands

10 9 8 7 6 5 4 3 2 1

ISBN 0-8050-0139-5

CONTENTS

INTRODUCTION

Paper is one of the most commonly used materials in daily life. Man has been using paper for thousands of years, and as yet it has not been replaced by any other material.

In the year 3000 BC the Egyptians were writing on the bark of the Papyrus plant and they continued to do so for the next four thousand years. The actual invention of paper as we know it is generally attributed to the Chinese in the second century AD.

The importance of paper for the purposes of communication and the dissemination of knowledge is obvious, and this aspect became even more widespread with the invention of printing.

In many societies paper has also acquired an essential role in cultural expression and as an artistic medium for local traditions.

For example, paper cut-out patterns from Poland are well known for their vitality and imagination and are considered as a form of folk art.

In Mexico, paper is used in many festive celebrations to make bunting, pinatas and numerous other cardboard and paper constructions which are used in colourful processions.

In Japan, paper was used for many different purposes, partly from economic necessity and partly for traditional reasons. Paper can be an effective material and it is cheap and generally easily available. The inherently sensitive nature of Japanese people has produced a variety of paper articles which are remarkable for their artistic quality as well as for their sense of humour. The art of paper folding is a favourite pastime of both children and adults in Japan.

Many years ago the art of making silhouettes was stimulated by monasteries throughout Europe. Today there is a revival of the creative use of paper in Western Europe, following the Japanese example. There are shops specialising in paper equipment, selling beautiful kites, for example. Not only the practical aspects of paper are considered, but also the ways in which it can be used as a hobby.

This book by Jack Botermans shows how paper and its rather coarser brother, cardboard, have provided endless pleasure for many people. It is about the elevated art of making something from virtually nothing, something attractive or amusing or surprising. The artistic element depends largely on your skill and dexterity, and all the models and toys in this book are a fascinating challenge. The book is aimed at those who are passionate about puzzles and games, who need only a sheet of paper or a piece of cardboard – plus a pair of scissors or a utility knife – to turn a dream into a reality. The reality will be fantastic objects created from next to nothing: a floating pyramid, strange dice, magnificent 3-d stars, and puzzles both ancient and modern – with objects like these, you enter the realms of magic.

TOOLS AND MATERIALS

What sort of paper is best to use, and what tools do you need? These are important questions and we will attempt to answer them below.

Paper

You will need a number of different sorts of paper. Obviously no one will mind if you simply tear a sheet off the nearest pad of paper, but there are many different kinds you can use. Not only the thickness of the paper is important, but also the actual structure. Paper can have a rough surface, it can be transparent or veined. Thus the type of paper you use depends on what you are going to do with it. With regard to the strength of your construction, it goes without saying that this depends to a great extent on the quality of paper you use. Always remember this.

Tools

For most of the objects described in this book you need only a few household tools or kitchen and garden implements. You won't have to buy any special equipment, though some people might consider that a stapler falls into this category. However, if you don't have a stapler, ordinary pins will do just as well. Clothespins or paperclips are used to hold the glued surfaces together while the glue dries, and you will need scissors of various types and sizes. There is a wide variety of tape, utility knives and glue. In most cases you will find all these in the home, and when you start to build the models described in this book you will only need to go shopping for the actual paper, perhaps some paint and... this book. It really couldn't be cheaper.

This page shows a number of the tools you will need to make the models described in this book:

Ruler
Scissors
Utility knife
Blunt — ended paring knife (for scoring lines)
Pencils and crayons
Felt tip pens
Stapler
Paperclips
Pins
Clothespins
Cellophane/plastic tape (such as Scotch ®tape)

ICE TEMPERED

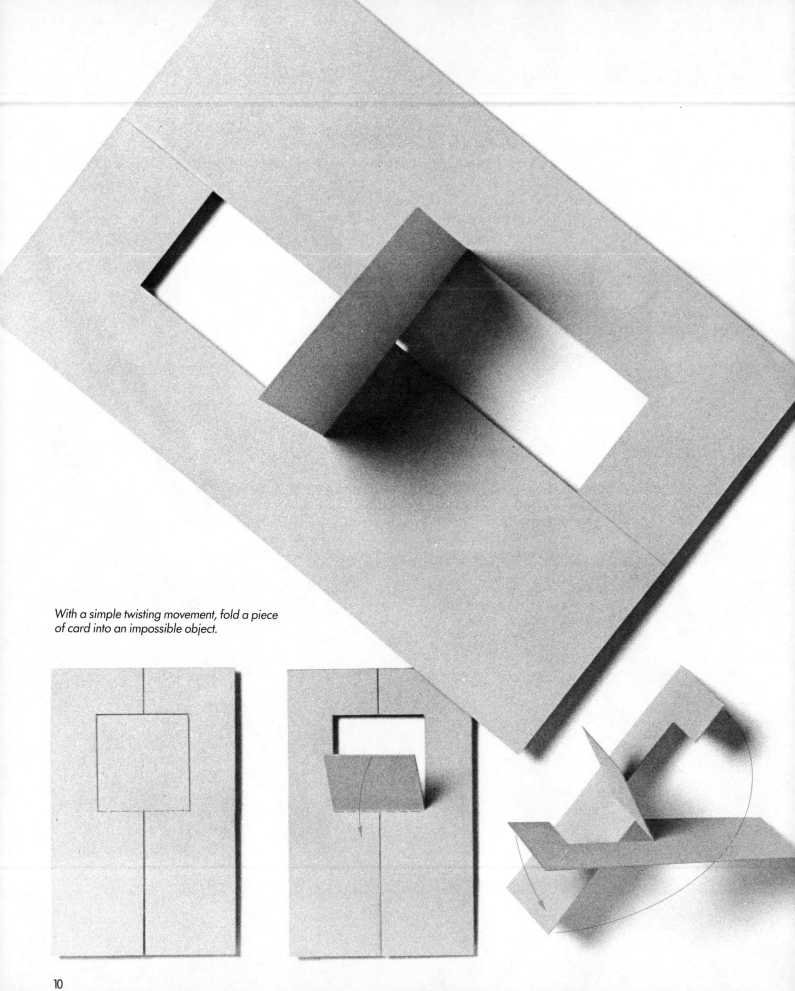

With a simple twisting movement, fold a piece
of card into an impossible object.

THE IMPOSSIBLE OBJECT 1

This idea is rather like a joke which is suddenly being told everywhere, in pubs and cafés throughout the land, in cities and country villages, though no one has any idea who told it first or where it originated.

This is rather unfortunate for the person who first thought of the joke – always assuming that it was a good one – for even if he got only a penny each time it was told, he would be able to retire on it.

In fact these 'impossible constructions' created with little bits of paper are very similar. Who thought of them first? Perhaps a father trying to impress his sons by making an impossible sculpture using no more than a piece of card folded and cut in an extremely ingenious way. This might be the answer, but there's really no way of finding out the truth. These creations simply suddenly appeared to amuse both those who were making them and those who merely stood around watching.

It's certainly advisable for a beginner to use card which has a pattern or structure on it so that you can camouflage the folds and cuts more easily. A utility knife can be used to score the lines of the folds first, and this is an essential tool for anyone making these structures.

When you have cut the centre piece, as in this example, and scored along the lines, the model can be folded into the right shape by simply turning it on its axis. It may be simple, but at the same time it's very puzzling.

To make the construction look even more puzzling you must camouflage the places where the folded cardboard comes together as much as you can. This can be done by decorating the construction or otherwise by rubbing out the cut slightly with a blunt object.

If you wish to perfect the actual presentation of your 'impossible' structure, it can be placed under a glass dome or in a lucite box so that no one can touch it.

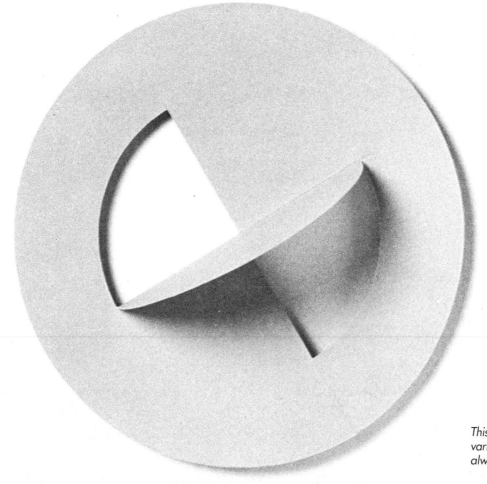

This round model forms an interesting variation on the rectangular 'miracle'. It is always possible to camouflage the cuts.

A WORK OF ART CONSISTING OF TETRAHEDRA

We will begin by explaining exactly what a tetrahedron is, as you might be under the impression that this term refers to a recently discovered species of dinosaur. This is certainly not the case. As any mathematician will tell you, a tetrahedron is a regular structure which consists of four equilateral triangles. The strip of card shown at the bottom of the following page consists of ten of these tetrahedra. This is a very special strip, as you will soon see if you examine it carefully.

You can twist the circle which can be made from this strip around its own axis to produce an extremely interesting effect, especially when the strip is painted in different bright colours.

This is merely one of the many possibilities. Obviously you don't need to make exactly ten tetrahedra – eight will do just as well, though this evidently restricts the possibilities to some extent. However, it's just as much fun making one of these special circles with ten as with eight tetrahedra.

Of course, you could always make a circle with twenty tetrahedra. This is even more fun because it means you can make a knot in the strip to produce a wonderful sight when you play around with the circle. The strips are very suitable for use as a bracelet or to give someone as a present, but a really ingenious person could use this standard model to make an extremely original work of art. There are plenty of possibilities to work with.

To make a ring of ten tetrahedra you need a piece of card 16 × 4 inch with an approximate thickness of 0.1 inch. The card should be folded meticulously. First score the lines with a utility knife. When you have cut everything out and scored all the lines as shown in the diagram, fold along the lines, bending the card forwards and backwards a few times. The order of sticking down the tabs can be seen from the numbering, ie, stick No 1 down on No 1, No 2 on No 2, and so on. Remember that this should be done very accurately as otherwise you will end up with a disaster. Obviously the way in which you decorate the circle, by painting it or gluing decorations on, is entirely up to you. The more colourful your circle is, the more exciting it will look.

This flat strip of card is transformed with a few folds and some glue into a genuine work of art.

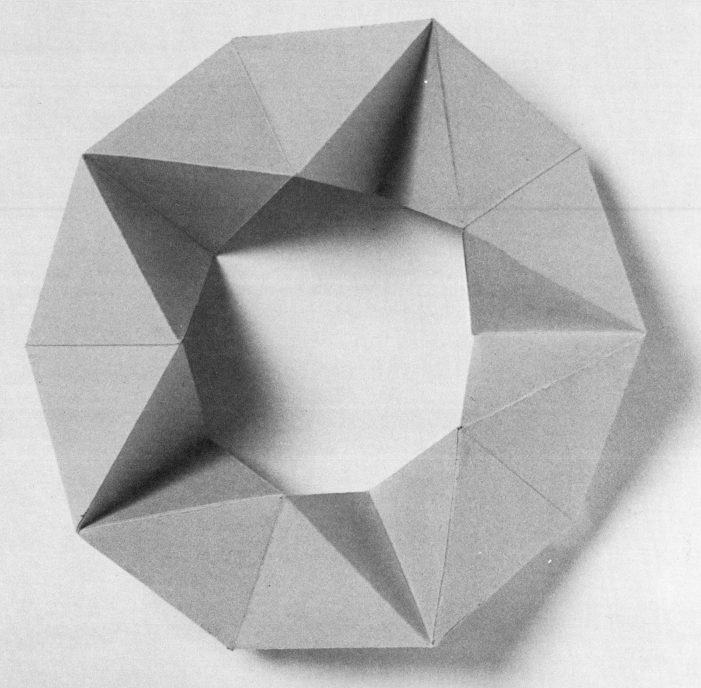

This circle of tetrahedra looks really difficult to make, but you will see that it is actually fairly simple.
Moreover, you won't be the only one to be surprised by the results – all your friends will be impressed as well.

The cube will snap shut with considerable force. This may give the person receiving it rather a shock but this is soon followed by a lovely surprise.

14

A SNAPPER

Here comes the postman bringing a mysterious parcel wrapped in brown paper. What a surprise and what fun to send someone a surprise like this. They'll wonder if it's a box of chocolates or possibly a book ordered so long ago that they've forgotten all about it.

They try and undo the knots in the string with impatient fingers, nervously tear the tough wrapping paper when suddenly... The mysterious thing they wonderingly unwrapped snaps shut and a cube appears in their hands. This could bear some sort of original message from the sender or the notification of a change of address, an invitation to a birthday party or New Year best wishes. If you want to make your own snapper and you want to make sure that your message is read, you could make your own cube, for example, one decorated with photographs of yourself and your family or with your own drawings. Don't imagine for a moment that a cube like this is difficult to make – it's actually very straightforward.

To make a cube 3.5 × 3.5 × 3.5 inch you need a piece of card 9 inch wide by 19 inch long. Make sure that the card is at least 0.3 inch thick. Copy the design shown here onto the piece of card. Cut out or cut the model and score the lines which need folding with the blunt edge of a pair of scissors or with a blunt paring knife. The whole model is stuck together as shown in the second example.

The tube on one side of the structure gives additional strength to the design. The most difficult part of the exercise is the next step, which can be rather fiddly, though an ordinary rubber band will be a great help. Finish by showing the message on the cube, and there you are!

These two stages show how this snapper cube is made.

A FLEXICUBE

Inventors are extraordinary people. When looking for one thing they often end up unexpectedly inventing something totally different. Mr A.H. Stone, an English mathematician who was studying in the United States, was someone like this. He was researching equilateral triangles made of flexible material when he chanced upon the cube described in this chapter.

Stone immediately realised the attractive aspects of this puzzle, for by chance he had managed to turn it inside out completely without using so much as a pair of scissors or a pot of glue. Then he wondered whether the average puzzler would be able to do this too.

It soon became obvious that the average person certainly couldn't manage this and the odd individual who did succeed took quite a long time over it. The flexicube turned out to be quite a complicated puzzle which made great demands on anyone keen on puzzles, let alone a complete amateur.

Obviously you can make the flexicube of paper or card, and if we were strictly adhering to the title of this book it certainly should be made of paper, but there is no reason why another material shouldn't be used. For example, this puzzle is very attractive when made of tin joined together on the inside with tape in such a way that there is enough room to fold between the corners. If you find this difficult to follow, there is a diagram showing the simple construction of a flexicube made of card or paper.

To make the flexicube, use a strip of card approximately 3 × 9 inch. Copy all the lines shown in the diagram onto this card. Now score along all these lines with a utility knife. To make a really flexible, easy-to-manipulate flexicube it is a good idea to bend the card backwards and forwards along these lines a few times.

Before sticking the strip of card into the shape of a cube with tape, it is advisable to give the sides of the cube a particular colour. This depends entirely on your own taste – a bright red, a subdued blue, a glaring yellow – whatever you like best. The coloured sides make it easier to see later on whether you have really succeeded in turning the flexicube inside out. This might otherwise be rather doubtful. Before we go on to the next example and forget to tell you how to turn the flexicube inside out, this is how to do it: first press the two corners A together to form a flat square in which – as shown in the illustration – the bottom corners are also folded towards each other (1). Then fold corners B towards each other to make a triangle (2). A square is produced when you then press in the corners C (3). Now pull out point D and fold the whole thing flat. Do the same with point D at the back of figure 4. You are now exactly halfway, so don't give up. Make another flat square and fold the corners E in (5). Turn the square around and pull the corners D out to make another flat square.

Now pull it all open – there you are. You can put everything back in its original form by reversing the process.

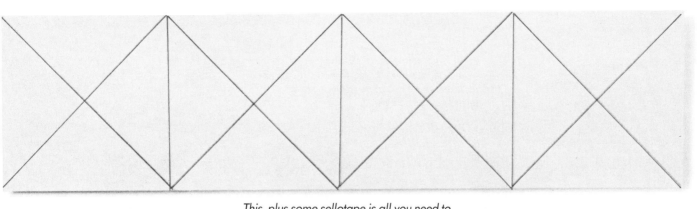

This, plus some sellotape is all you need to make this puzzle.

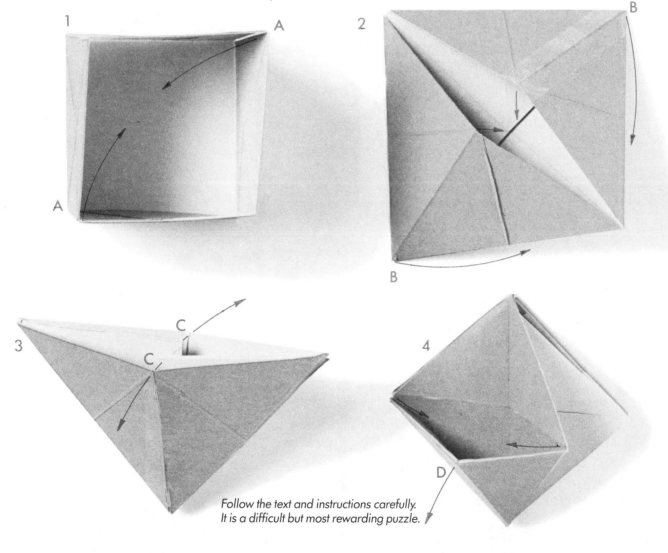

1 A

A

2 B

B

3 C

C

4 D

Follow the text and instructions carefully. It is a difficult but most rewarding puzzle.

5 E

E

6 F

F

In his 'Encyclopaedia of Puzzles', which dates from 1914, Sam Lloyd calls this puzzle 'a royal success'. There are three solutions to it including Lloyd's own.

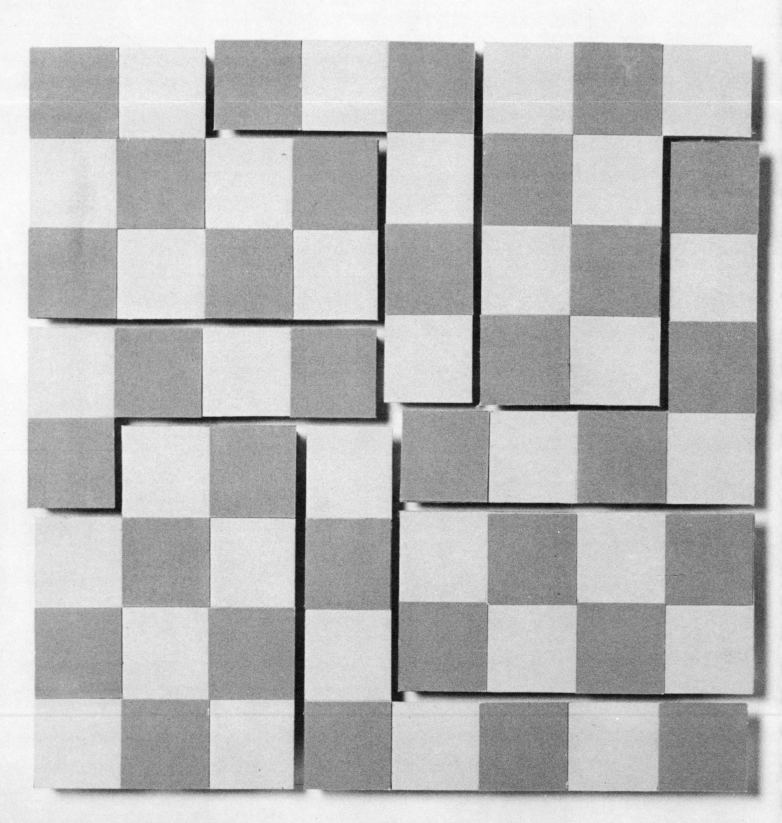

THE DIVIDED CHESSBOARD

At first sight this divided chessboard looks very simple; a puzzle which you would imagine could be solved in a few seconds. However appearances are deceptive. Researching the background to this puzzle, Jerry Slocum, who compiled a short book of chess puzzles, came across a remarkable quotation by a certain Professor Hoffman.

In 1893 this scientist had already warned against the deceptive simplicity of the solution of this puzzle, 'until you find that you have space left for only three pieces, while you are still holding six in your hands...' Quite possibly Hoffman spent many fruitless evenings attempting to solve the mystery of this puzzle with its double bottom.

Slocum also discovered that a patent had been taken out on the puzzle in September 1880 for the United States of America. The person taking out this patent was Henry Buers, who considered that the puzzle was such a pleasant way of whiling away long winter evenings that this was in itself a good enough reason for popularising it.

Buers probably thought that he'd struck gold – like those who invented Scrabble® and Monopoly® – but this turned out to be a disappointment, probably because the divided chessboard was too easy to make.

Take a piece of cardboard approximately 6.5 inch square and draw a chequered pattern on it with squares 0.8 × 0.8 inch. To make it look like a chessboard the squares are coloured alternately black and white. Obviously you can use felt tip pens to do this, but a more professional look is usually obtained if you stick pieces of black paper on every other square. Then you cut out the pieces in the pattern shown here. This is based on eight pieces, but there is absolutely no reason why you should not make your own version. If you do this you must assume that fifteen pieces is the maximum number for an attractive puzzle. To make it a little easier, you could also make a little box about 6.5 × 6.5 inch with the chequered pattern drawn onto it.

You can make a number of different versions of the Divided Chessboard. This is the version with thirteen pieces, designed by Gary Foshee.

THE MOBIUS STRIP

The Mobius strip is a miracle of simplicity named after Augustus Mobius, a German mathematician from the last century. The whole puzzle is no more than a piece of paper with one cut in it. The stroke of genius consists in the way it is twisted and the way in which the ends of the strip are stuck together (the bottom onto the top). You can no longer tell which is the inside and which is the outside. They seem to simply merge together.

The Mobius strip isn't used just to fascinate the audience. Try experimenting with it yourself and you'll be surprised by the results.

There is nothing so simple to make as a Mobius strip, but you must begin by deciding what sort you want to make. The easiest is a strip of paper with a cut down the middle. Then twist the strip through 360° and stick the ends together so that the top is stuck onto the bottom. With a bit of cutting you will find that you end up with two links of a chain entwined together.

However, this is not the only possibility. Provided the strip is long enough, it is possible to give it an extra twist, or just to twist it through 180°. If you now stick the ends together the effect is even stranger. This also applies to the strip with a cut which is not quite in the middle so that it has a wide and a narrow half.

Another nice idea is to use two Mobius strips together. If you then twist them and stick the ends together the results will be different again. There are countless possibilities with the Mobius strip, some of which are quite unpredictable. For example, if you colour the halves in different colours, you will be delighted with the effect, which has an almost magical quality. This is even further enhanced when you use a number of strips with half twists as well as whole and double twists. It's not for nothing that conjurors wax lyrical about the possibilities of the magical Mobius strip.

UNKNOWN UPHILL FORCES

Surely this isn't possible? If you think that, you're wrong. This cone seems to roll uphill, as though one of the works of the graphic artist M.C. Escher has come to life. In his drawings Escher even managed to suggest that water could flow uphill. This cone, which rolls uphill, is perhaps not quite as spectacular, but nevertheless...

Perhaps it isn't really rolling uphill. Is it an optical illusion, just like Escher's work? The truth of the matter is that it is, and the observer is taken for a ride. If you look closely, you will see that in reality the cone is rolling downhill. The strange 'track', the triangle on which the cone rolls, as well as the cone itself, are so sophisticated that the cone seems to roll uphill.

You could compare it to a mountain road. When you have gone up for a while, on your bike, or, in greater comfort, in your car, you will notice just before you get to the top that the road seems to run down again. This is an illusion, and if you then decide to shift into neutral gear, you will see that you will start rolling back down.

The phenomenon never ceases to amaze, just like the cone.

The cone consists of two separate cones stuck together and made as shown in the diagram below. To ensure that it will roll smoothly, the lip which serves to stick the two parts together, should not be folded. You must first score along the indented side of the cone with a utility knife to make a really sharp angle. The two cones can then be stuck together along this indented edge.

The track which the cone rolls 'up' is made of a strip of card. You must do this exactly in accordance with the sizes given, otherwise the 'illusion' will not work. Lastly, although the examples in this book are always made with paper and card, as the title suggests, there is no reason why this cone, which rolls uphill, should not be made of wood. However, in this case it should be turned wood, and this is not as easy for an amateur to produce. All the same, it's certainly worthwhile making an attempt.

The sides of these figures should be followed exactly.

22

It looks like a solution to the energy problem.
You won't believe your eyes when you see the
cone rolling uphill under its own steam.

Onlookers will stare in wonder and incredulity.
How is it possible? This is the impossible
made real.

24

You won't believe your eyes and you'll find yourself staring at something quite impossible for minutes on end, your forehead wrinkled in incomprehension. The more you turn it round and round, the more difficult it is to understand. Higher forces must have been at work. Perhaps the work of the Great Magician himself.

If you want to be the star attraction at any party, this is the birthday present to give, preferably presented in a sturdy lucite box which is impossible to open. Superglue is the ideal adhesive for this purpose. Your present will undoubtedly be the main talking point of the evening and you will find that everyone will want to know the secret of this 'impossible' object.

The secret lies mainly in the legerdemain which is so popular amongst conjurors. No matter how carefully you look, you can't see everything. For example, you can't see the places where the card has been cut, or was it folded, or where the cuts merge into folds, or are they really just cuts?

Obviously it requires extreme accuracy to make this impossible object, but once you've completed it, you'll find you can't wait to do another.

Of course, it's always possible to make this impossible object from a business card that someone's just given you. You'll find that this is always a great success.

But if it's the first time that you're trying one, it's best to make a slightly larger model. On the other hand, don't make one of giant proportions or an observant onlooker will soon be able to fathom the secret.

It's a good idea to start with an 'impossible object' measuring about 6 × 6 inch. Use card roughly 0.2 inch thick and try to find card which has the same sort of surface on both sides. This surface, like the decoration you can add later, makes it even more possible to trick the observer and to hide the secret cuts and folds in such a way that they are invisible to the human eye.

Carefully follow the three examples given below and erase any guidelines you have drawn. If you have a pair of folding scissors, this is obviously an advantage in making one of these 'eyecatchers' from a business card.

MOVING HOUSE

Have you ever moved house? If not, don't start now because there's nothing as depressing as moving house. It can drive you quite crazy. One minute you can be holding a valuable vase in your hand, the next it has disappeared. General panic follows. You can't remember whether it's actually in the removal van, or where exactly – it might even still be in the attic with the other junk. It all leads to quarrelling and remarks like: 'Why don't you think when you put things down?' In other words, moving house is one of the worst things that can happen to you. However, this certainly isn't true of the moving house puzzle, which is really good fun. Although it won't come as a great surprise that the man who first dreamed up this puzzle, J.H. Flemming, was once a removal man. No one else could have thought of such a thing. You really have to have a streak of the devil in you to come up with this one.

Just imagine that you have a livingroom and in this livingroom there is a grand piano. This has undoubtedly been the most unpopular article of furniture with removal men since Stan Laurel and Oliver Hardy dragged one down a steep flight of stairs. Fortunately the piano in this puzzle doesn't have to leave the room. Once you've got it in the door, you've succeeded in doing the puzzle. However, this is not so simple, as there is quite a bit of furniture in the room already. As all the other articles of furniture are just as heavy as the piano, and you are quite alone, you'll have to do a fair bit of rearranging. The cupboard can go in the corner and the piano comes forward. Then the piano can be moved further forward still, so that the cupboard can go behind it, and this will make some room for the table. Or might it be better to put the table there so that the chair can be moved to the right? Or perhaps there's another more sensible way of doing it. You'll soon realize that it can drive you completely round the twist, just like moving house can, but at least you'll never lose anything when doing this moving house puzzle – we hope.

The moving house puzzle is fairly easy to make yourself. You'll need two pieces of card. The card should be at least 0.1 inch thick. The first piece is used to make a box representing the room, and the second piece of card (4 × 4.5 inch) is used to make the furniture, as shown in the diagram.

It's a good idea to round off the corners of the furniture by filing them with a nail file. This means they will be easier to slide past each other. Label the pieces so that you know what each represents, or stick a picture on each piece of furniture concerned. More creative people can

A good training for anyone who's contemplating moving house: the moving house puzzle.

even paint the pieces.

The remaining edge is used as the plinth for the living-room, which is folded from the first piece of card. Use a good quality adhesive, for there's nothing so ugly as crooked walls. Obviously it's possible to put wallpaper on the walls, but this is certainly not essential. Now you are ready to try and move the piano towards the opening of the door. You can move just one piece at a time, and you can't lift the pieces or slide them over each other. Obviously you should use the starting position shown opposite.

The edge of the piece of card used to cut out the pieces of furniture can serve as the plinth for the living-room where the removal takes place.

Just for fun, it's possible to draw the articles of furniture concerned on your pieces.

CATCHING THE SWAN

You'll sometimes come across a dogcatcher in old American comic strips:
a rather dopey figure driving around in a dilapidated van with an assortment
of nets. But the dogcatchers in these comics don't seem to do very well. Either
they are bitten on the backside by giant bulldogs or they get tangled up in their
own enormous nets. So we have chosen a far safer piece of equipment – a
sliding cage – to try to trap a swan.
This sliding cage is easy to make yourself and the swan can be folded in the
origami style.

*Catch the swan. Use some cardboard and a
swan folded in the origami style to make a
fun-to-do sliding puzzle.*

This pattern clearly shows the individual parts making up the puzzle.

This puzzle is made of two pieces of card 12 × 12 inch. The card should be at least 0.1 inch thick and one of the sheets should be divided up as shown in the diagram. The edge will be stuck down on the other piece of card later on. The middle piece, which is cut in various rectangles and squares, automatically forms the sliding pieces. Smooth these pieces round the side with fine sandpaper so that they slide more easily. The rectangle left over at the end when the other pieces have been cut out, forms the walls, and these are stuck down vertically on the second sheet of card, which thus becomes the sliding tray. Now only the swan remains to be made. A sheet of writing paper 8 × 12 inch will do. Follow the instructions in the diagram precisely and, hey presto, you have a swan. This is then glued down on the large square of card. The puzzle consists in catching the bird in the cage by cleverly sliding the pieces around.

Origami. This traditional method of folding paper is used to make a swan, which is then placed in the puzzle.

TANGRAM: THE PUZZLE AS AN ART FORM

No one knows exactly where Tangram originated. Obviously it was in China, but that is as much as anyone can tell you. The American puzzle expert, Sam Lloyd, seemed to have solved the secret of Tangram many years ago. At any rate he published an entire treatise to show that this game, which had suddenly gained widespread popularity, was actually thought up by the Chinese god, Tan. Lloyd even referred to the seven holy books of Tan, which were purported to contain about ten thousand illustrations of figures which can be made with Tangram. These ten thousand illustrations supposedly represented the story of the Creation.

Later research revealed that Mr. Lloyd must have had a very active imagination. He had even brought in such learned figures as Archimedes and Pythagoras to lend credibility to his theories. Even his so-called 'Tanka girls', who were supposed to have amused sailors with these games in the port of Canton, proved to be figments of his imagination.

Thus Tangram was once again imbued with the spirit of mystery. At the beginning of the nineteenth century the game suddenly became universally popular, and it is even said that Napoleon lightened his last days with the game. Tangram is a game that consists of seven pieces, made by dividing up a square in a particular way. These parts are put together in such a way that they make all sorts of different figures, the shapes of people and animals, as well as many different artefacts, figures and letters.

Tangram is very easy to make, particularly if you follow the instructions in the diagram very accurately. First, choose the material you are going to use. If this is to be a piece of thick card – suitable for a first attempt – the best size to choose is 4 × 4 inch. On the card draw 16 squares of equal size (see the example), and through these, the thicker lines shown on the diagram. You then cut up the piece of card along the lines shown in the diagram. This inevitably results in one square, a parallelogram (a sort of lopsided square), and five triangles – two large ones, one medium sized one, and two smaller ones. These pieces should be cut out by drawing a sharp knife along a metal ruler. The Tans, the actual pieces of the Tangram, will be nice and sharp if you do this. Obviously the Tans can be decorated in all sorts of ways.

It cannot be denied that Sam Lloyd added a large number of new figures to Tangram. He must have been quite obsessed with the game. For example, he thought up figures representing two different things, depending on the point of view from which they were regarded. A real Tangram enthusiast will always be on the lookout for this sort of figure, but to be honest, it is virtually impossible to come up with any new figures now.

Nevertheless, Tangram is still a game with a remarkable number of possibilities. It's not for nothing that the Chinese call Tangram 'the board of wisdom'. You can make an amazing number of different figures from these seven simple shapes: plump or skinny animals, letters as well as numbers.

Tangram requires a great deal of imagination; and apparently there is even a book on mathematics in which the various geometrical shapes are shown in pieces of Tangram.

Tangram can be viewed as a sort of science, but it can also be considered as an art form. Poets and painters have been inspired by Tangram. They were quite fascinated by this strange game in which pieces which are in themselves so simple and angular are used to make delicate figures. In fact, the pieces themselves can be very artistic. They are sometimes made from beautifully carved wood, or from bone or ivory. In some cases the games are actually extremely valuable works of art.

You can make all sorts of jumping, dancing figures with the seven Tans.

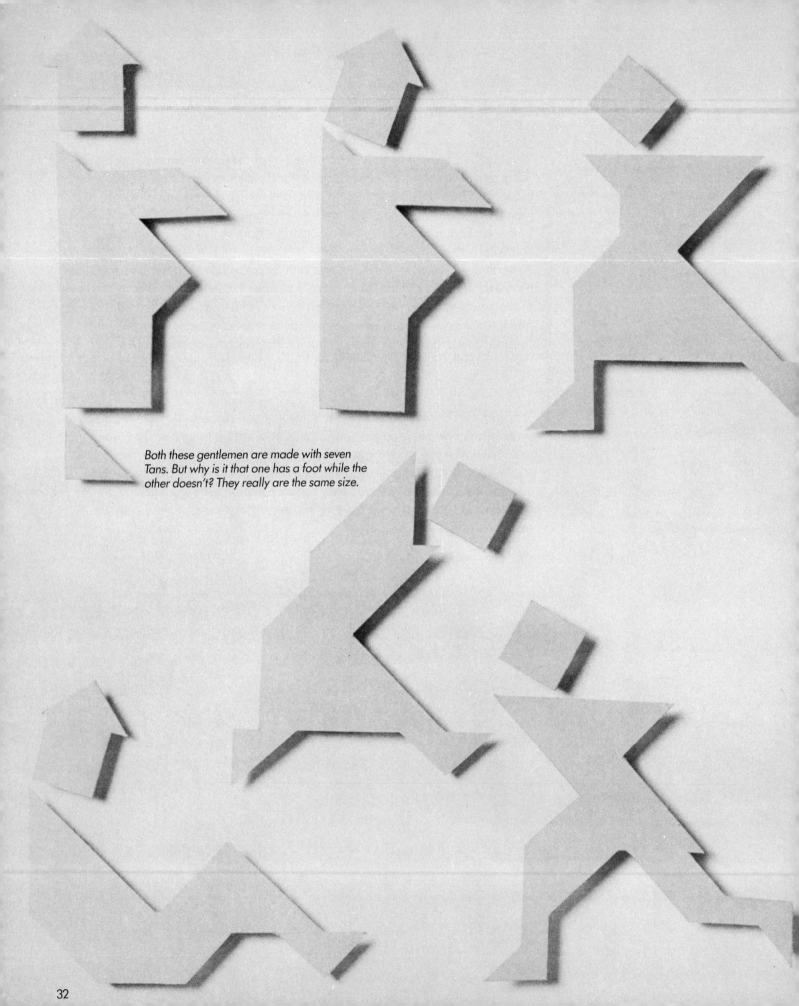

Both these gentlemen are made with seven Tans. But why is it that one has a foot while the other doesn't? They really are the same size.

Try copying these figures. It may prove to be
quite difficult, but it's certainly not impossible.

Try copying these figures. It may prove to be quite difficult, but it's certainly not impossible.

Van Deventer thought of this intricate puzzle.
You can spend hours making it.

38

MATCHBOXES BY VAN DEVENTER

You probably learned your first matchbox trick at a very early age. Slide a full box upside down in the sleeve and it's great fun to watch an unsuspecting member of the family open the box next time. If he opens it with the top facing up – which is more than likely as the force of habit is great – the matches will be scattered all over the floor before he knows where he is!

This is all great fun for a three year old, though no three year old will be able to cope with this advanced matchbox puzzle, thought up quite recently by a young Dutchman, Oskar van Deventer. When Oskar was playing around with some empty matchboxes one day, he developed an extremely sophisticated as well as amusing puzzle, for which he used only five boxes.

With these five boxes he made five models and the game consisted simply of *shutting all the boxes.* This puzzle was published in the Dutch newspaper, the *NRC Handelsblad,* by Leon Vie, who delighted in this fiendishly simple but terrible trick.

All you need are five matchboxes and a tube of good adhesive. The length, width and height measurements should be in the ratio 3:2:1, and the best matchboxes to use are those which measure 1.8 × 1.2 × 0.6 inch, as these comply with this ratio. Glue the boxes together in the way shown in the illustration.

There are actually three ways of sliding the boxes together, and we will provide the hapless reader with one solution, leaving him to find the other two for himself. Remember that there are also incorrect solutions. It cannot be denied that matchboxes are fairly flexible, and there are those who manage to push the boxes into the sleeves by forcing them – this is a technique which can certainly not be condoned. In other words, any solutions achieved in this way *do not count.*

All you need are 5 matchboxes in order to make this puzzle.

THE PIRATE FLAG

Imagine this. It's 1600, you're sailing off the coast of Dunkirk in an honourable vessel, when suddenly you see a strange galleon draw up alongside. Is it a pirate ship? They're certainly not unknown in these waters. You're ready to give them a broadside when you see that a 'friendly' flag is flying on the mast. It has eight stripes and happens to be that of a friendly nation.

All the orders are cancelled. The cannon are rolled back into place, the sailors start scrubbing the decks, the cook is rattling the pans in the galley when suddenly the flag with the eight stripes changes into a flag with nine stripes. And this is the flag of the infamous pirate, Jean Crévaison. Apparently he had also studied the puzzle with the pirate flag. This puzzle is one in which a 'friendly' flag can change in a fraction of a second into an enemy flag.

The flag with a false bottom. Follow the diagram exactly when you are making your pirate flag.

You make the pirate flag by drawing a flag with eight stripes on a piece of card 6 × 8 inch about 0.2 inch thick. The example shown here must be followed exactly. Then draw in the stepped diagonal exactly as shown in the example.

Cut out the flag which you have drawn already, with a penknife or scissors, and cut the pirate flag along the stepped diagonals. Then colour the flag any colour you wish and your pirate flag is finished. If you slide the right half down one step and then join the two halves, you will see that the flag which began with eight stripes now has nine stripes. Just what a clever pirate always needed.

BRAIN TEASER

It's almost impossible to imagine a more amusing puzzle. These puzzles pose almost insurmountable problems for anyone, and yet in principle even a three year old toddler could solve them. All you need is a flexible mind.
Take this brain teaser, for example. The object is to remove the string from the card without tearing or cutting it. Do you think that it's possible? The French say: *'Simple comme bonjour'*. In other words, 'It's as easy as pie'.

For this puzzle you'll need a piece of flexible card, a length of string and two large beads. If you like, you can also make two small cardboard pyramids to use instead of the beads. Take your pick. Cut two grooves across almost the entire length of the card with a sharp penknife. Then cut a third line at right angles to these grooves and now thread the string through the three cuts.

The puzzle is easy to make. Instead of beads you can use pieces of wood or piramids of cardboard.

If you now knot the two large beads at the end of the string (or your two cardboard pyramids), it seems impossible that you could pull the string through the card without tearing it badly. However, this is an illusion. It's not only possible, but actually very easy.

Almost there – just a few more moves to go.

The piramid laid out flat. You can attach them to the end of the strings.

PENTOMINOES

This is not a mathematics textbook, nor does it pretend to be one. But in dealing with pentominoes the reader will have to immerse himself in a number of geometrical shapes. If all this is not to become too complicated, he must be able to understand the many false bottoms which have made the pentomino a favourite amongst real puzzle enthusiasts.

'Pentomino' sounds like an advanced move in figure skating, but nothing could be further from the truth. A pentomino, hereafter referred to as a 'pento', is a shape which consists of five squares joined together. Perhaps this seems a rather enigmatic description, but don't forget that two squares joined together are known as a 'domino', the very piece used in the game of dominoes. When three of these squares are joined together in any shape you like, it's called a tromino, and when you have four squares, it's called a tetromino, so that five joined together will be a pentomino (pento). Just in case you're wondering, there's also a hexomino, consisting of six squares, but this is a bit more than most puzzle enthusiasts can handle. It can be used to make thirty-five different shapes, which is rather excessive.

A pento can be made into twelve different shapes. These twelve shapes – or building bricks, as it were – form respectively the letters I, L, P, T, U, V, W, X ,Y and Z, a rather lopsided F, and an N which doesn't really look like one. However, puzzle enthusiasts may be lacking in many ways, but never in imagination.

Right then. Twelve pentoes. Computer buffs will immediately realize that no fewer than 2339 rectangles can be made with sides of respectively six and ten squares. It should be remembered that in the solution there should not be any place where four pentoes have only one plane in common. Nor is it any good if the pentoes are placed in such a way that there is a straight dividing line from one side to the other of the pattern.

Any self-respecting puzzle freak will be itching to have a go, because the possibilities are endles.

Here we go then. Try making a pattern in the shape of a square with eight small squares on all sides. In the middle you can have a hole measuring two by two squares. It doesn't matter where. You think this is easy, don't you? Well, forget it. There are thousands of possibilities, and it is even more difficult if you want the hole to be in the centre, for there are only fifty-eight solutions.

Pentoes. There are cases on record of people who became so addicted to this phenomenon that they couldn't even stop for dinner.

These are the twelve pentoes. If you look closely, you can actually recognize the letters. However, it's more important to remember that every pento consists of five squares arranged into different patterns.

This square is made up of a complete set of pentoes. Try and think of some of the solutions yourself.

The wonderful thing about pentoes is that you can make the puzzle as complicated as you like. For example, try making a square with two halves that are exactly identical. One example of this is printed here, but remember that there are a

One of the things that appeals most to puzzle freaks is to make their own puzzles, especially when this is not too problematical. All you have to do to make this one is to trace the pieces shown here on a piece of card. Then simply cut out the pieces. Obviously you can make the pentoes as attractive as you wish by sanding and varnishing them.

number of different possible solutions. This is one of the really delightful aspects of the pento puzzle. You can find out for yourself exactly how many solutions there are.

For the figures shown here you need no more and no fewer than twelve pentoes. As you know, a pento consists of five squares, thus the entire pattern consists of sixty squares.

All the patterns shown here can be made with pentoes. Obviously the pentoes must not overlap. Don't stop when you've found one solution because there are always other solutions possible.

Any pento can be copied with nine other pentoes. If you don't believe it, look at the X shown below.

The first five patterns are chessboards gone wrong. Chessboards with four holes, each consisting of a single square. There are also some long, thin, short and thick rectangles of which the long thin one (three by twenty squares) is the most difficult. In fact, there are only two possible solutions to this one.

Of the last four models, the cross is by far the most difficult. However, with a little bit of ingenuity, you can solve this problem, just like the pento puzzle shown on this page. The principle is very simple. Choose a pento and copy it, using nine of the other pieces.

It's not an easy task, but it's great fun, especially as the results are always three times as long and as wide as the basic model. Believe it or not, whatever pento you use as a basic model, it can always be copied.

BANGERS

People are very funny creatures. If you're beating a carpet in your own front porch with a carpet beater, no one will give it a second thought. It's a familiar sound. But if you blow up a paper bag to bursting point and then punch it hard, unsuspecting passers-by will be cringing even before the echo of the bang has faded away. It's certainly a very old trick, but the joker with a paper bag can always produce the results he wants.

You can achieve the same effect with a piece of paper, and especially with a bill for example. Hold the sharp edge of the note against your lips, and blow while you make a tearing movement with one hand, sharp against the edge. This will really annoy your companions, but they'll be even more put out when you suddenly make the note bang. You really can do this – look at the diagram.

If you whip it down really fast, this simple toy will make a terrific bang.

Follow the instructions step by step to fold your banger.

All you need for this trifling sound production is a sheet of paper, e.g., from a writing pad. You fold this as shown in the example, to make a triangle. Hold the triangle between the thumb and index finger at the bottom, and with a quick flick of the wrist, whip it down. If you do it properly, you'll find this makes a loud bang.

If it doesn't work, try again with thicker paper, though it's also possible that you didn't 'whip' the triangle down correctly. This takes a little practice. In fact, the better you execute the whip, and the thicker the card, the louder the bang will be.

You'll have to copy the templates of the dice very accurately for the puzzle to work.

Make yourself an alternative to dice. You'll only need some strips of card.
When you've folded this model, you'll have to make two more folds along the dotted line in the direction of the arrow and glue down the last triangle.

HEXAFLEXAGON

We didn't think of this word, so don't blame us. We wouldn't have dared. The word is almost impossible to pronounce – a veritable tongue twister.

It's called a hexaflexagon and this word conceals a surprisingly flexible triangle discovered just before the Second World War by the English student of mathematics, A.H. Stone, who was doing research in the USA. As in most cases of 'great' inventions, the trusty Stone was looking for something quite different – but we won't hold that against him. After all, his discovery has led to a number of amusing puzzles, of which this is just one.

The Hexaflexagon shown here – and we'll try to make that the last time we use the word – consists of nineteen equilateral triangles. Fold all these as shown in the examples on these pages and you'll end up with a hexagon which turns round on its own axis. This is a nice little toy for us, but for Mr A.H. Stone it was merely the first step into the mysterious and amazing world of the Hex...

At first sight this game looks rather complicated to make. But what is complicated? This Hexaflexagon certainly isn't. All you need is a long strip of thick paper or thin card. For the model in our example we've used a strip of card about 16 inch long and 1.6 inch wide. But provided that you stick to this ratio, you can use any strip as long or as short as you like. Copy the model shown here accurately and score all the fold lines so that all the edges will be as sharp as possible. Then fold the whole thing in the way shown in the example. Make the last folds along the dotted line. As you will see, one of the nineteen triangles will remain, and this triangle can be glued against the opposite triangle.

Now the model is finished, but to make the whole thing more interesting, you could cover it with spots, as in our example, or colour it. If you use the dots

the structure will look like an alternative to dice; if you use colours, make sure you use six different colours.

FOLDING, FOLDING

Obviously this is not merely a question of folding simple little squares willy-nilly. In fact, one might suppose that this pastime had some connections with higher mathematics, as well as with art. Certainly paper folding is not a new phenomenon, and the history of this art dates back over two thousand years.

You start with a square of paper divided into sixteen squares with a few dots and cuts here and there. These dots form an awkward but quite amusing problem, ie, to fold the paper in such a way that the squares with the same number of dots come to be opposite each other.

We've made two variations on this puzzle, one of which is simpler than the other. For the first puzzle, divide a piece of paper 4 × 4inch into sixteen squares. Score along the lines with a utility knife and make three grooves in the places shown on the diagram. Fold the paper backwards and forwards along all the lines and show the right number of dots on the model. Dot this exactly according to the example – otherwise attempting the solution to the puzzle will be a hopeless proposition before you even start.

The second puzzle is rather more difficult. This is because of the square hole in the middle. Again it is obviously essential to copy the dots in exactly the right squares.

A puzzle to get your teeth into. You'll alternate between total despair and brief periods of elation. There's no better present you could make for a friend.

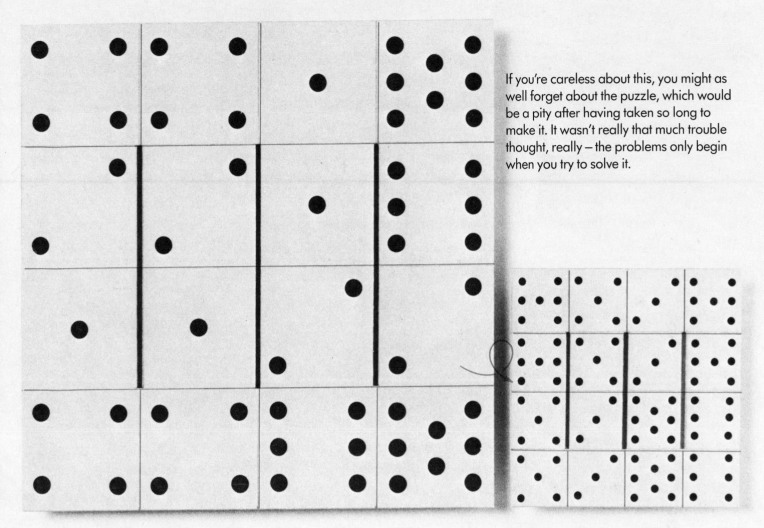

If you're careless about this, you might as well forget about the puzzle, which would be a pity after having taken so long to make it. It wasn't really that much trouble thought, really — the problems only begin when you try to solve it.

Follow the pattern of dots in this example exactly. As you can see, there is a front and a back for most models.

Suggestion. There's a wonderful variation that you could make of the second puzzle. Cut the square 'ring' on one side with a pair of scissors or a utility knife and turn it through 180°. Then join it together again with tape. You'll soon realize that this makes the puzzle twice as difficult. Whether it also makes the puzzle twice as much fun to do depends entirely on your capacity to persevere.

THE ILLUSION OF REALITY

Don't be afraid to deny that you too have been tricked by this simple illusion. It's an optical joke that we've all played on one another at some time. You take a pencil and a piece of paper and draw two lines exactly the same lenght. One of the lines has arrows at the end pointing inwards and the other has the arrows pointing outwards. The question is: which of the two lines is the longer?

This could be called an optical illusion, and the graphic artist from Leeuwarden, M.C. (Maurits Cornelis) Escher, was a master of this type of optical illusion. In his woodcuts and lithographs he managed to show water running uphill and produced all sorts of other conjuring tricks with perspective that made him world famous.

The designer of the optical illusion shown here was undoubtedly inspired by Escher's work, and you could try copying them in card; at least you could make an attempt, because there are quite a few pitfalls on the way. The two crooked figures below may not be utterly impossible, but what about the figure opposite?

Can you dot it or can't you? Is it possible or not? If you can't do it, I'd like to assure you that we managed. Don't give up too quickly. Perhaps we're putting you on. Conjuring tricks with perspective are quite fascinating, but sometimes you really feel that your mind is becoming addled.

To design these figures we used three Swedish postage stamps as examples. Again the question arises: can they be copied or not? Have a go.

SVERIGE 25   SVERIGE 50   SVERIGE 75

*We're not going to tell you how we did it –
we're only going to say that it's actually
possible – or perhaps it isn't.*

PICK A NUMBER

In the middle of a conversation, try casually interjecting: 'Hey, guess what I've just found out. I'm clairvoyant.' The chances are that the listeners will immediately demand proof. This won't present any problems. Ask someone to think of a number under sixty and to prevent the others from thinking that it's all a big hoax, he can whisper the number to them.

Now you take out your number cards. These are cards showing a few different numbers. You ask the subject the obvious question: Is the number you're thinking of on this card? If the answer is negative, put the card to one side. If the answer is affirmative, remember the first number on the card. When you've shown your victim all the cards, you have to do some lightning mental arithmetic for you will have to add up all the first numbers on the cards on which the subject saw his secret number. The result of this addition is the number that the subject had in mind. Does this seem rather far-fetched? You might think so at first sight, but it's true and your audience will not discover that you're not really clairvoyant until you tell them the secret. Let them discover it for themselves.

It couldn't be easier to make the strips which you need for this performance. A large piece of card about 0.4 inch thick is divided into six strips 12 inch long and 1.2 inch wide. Of course, you can also make them smaller, but if you want to perform to a large audience, it's best not to make the cards too small. Then write down the figures shown here, neatly and clearly on the cards and you're ready for the opening night.

You can use these strips to give a performance as a clairvoyant. Make them now.

Whether you make the strips large or small doesn't really matter, but make sure that you copy the numbers correctly.

1	2	4	8	16	32
3	3	5	9	17	33
5	6	6	10	18	34
7	7	7	11	19	35
9	10	12	12	20	36
11	11	13	13	21	37
13	14	14	14	22	38
15	15	15	15	23	39
17	18	20	24	24	40
19	19	21	25	25	41
21	22	22	26	26	42
23	23	23	27	27	43
25	26	28	28	28	44
27	27	29	29	29	45
29	30	30	30	30	46
31	31	31	31	31	47
33	34	36	40	48	48
35	35	37	41	49	49
37	38	38	42	50	50
39	39	39	43	51	51
41	42	44	44	52	52
43	43	45	45	53	53
45	46	46	46	54	54
47	47	47	47	55	55
49	50	52	56	56	56
51	51	53	57	57	57
53	54	54	58	58	58
55	55	55	59	59	59
57	58	60	60	60	60
59	59				

95

FLYING WITH PAPER

Building a plane? This art is almost as old as paper itself. There are scores of ways of turning a sheet of paper into all sorts of advanced models of planes. The planes will really fly throught the air for a matter of seconds before crashing down to earth in a graceful arc after a long glide. Usually they crash somewhere you'd never have expected – in the middle of the daffodils, for example, or into the cat's whiskers as it lies dozing in the sun.

Entire books have been devoted to building paper airplanes, including *Paper Flight* (Henry Holt and Company). We have made a combination of different planes, together forming a new, futuristic box, though whether this rocket-like toy can really be termed a box is a debatable point. Even real airplane builders will find themselves admiring this beautifully assembled model.

For the main body of this plane you'll need a sheet of paper 8 × 12 inch, folded double and then opened out again. Then make two points by folding in the two top corners along the dotted line, and repeat this as shown in the model. Now fold the entire plane double and staple the wings down at the arrow after first pulling them down slightly. Fold the back of the plane back in and up along the dotted line so that there is a so-called 'stabilo'.

These little paper airplanes will conjure up the magic of youth.

Now for the wings. For these you need another sheet of paper 8 × 12 inch. Fold it along the diagonals shown. It's a good idea to fold the paper backwards and forwards a few times.

Now fold the sheet in two lengthways, at the same time pressing in the corners on the diagonals. If you have done this properly, you will see the shape of the wings emerging. Fold the left side, ie, the front of the wing, lightly down and make a small cut in the back, as shown in the example. The four separate points now need to be folded in along the dotted line.

This is a sort of wing in which the top layer is folded straight up at both ends. These are the stabilizers. Now glue the front edge of the wing together. Assemble the whole plane by gluing the main part of the body and the wing together as shown in the example. Ready for take off.

If you want the planes to be really aerodynamic, follow the instructions carefully.

MULTIPLES

Multiples are paper airplanes which are an absolute delight for any real enthusiast. Ten of these wings are joined together. Try making one yourself. If you get it right you'll produce an unforgettable spectacle. It may sound unbelievable, but you can make these multiples 1 yard long. Of course, this means you will need six wings or tailpieces, or whatever you choose to call these pieces.

However, the pieces themselves require some description. At first sight the way in which these multiples are constructed looks fairly simple. But the folding instructions must be followed very accuraely – even if you're only a few milli-metres out, your plane will undoubtedly crash to the ground only seconds after you have launched it in the air.

The step-by-step process for making this plane starts with the nose. This is made from a sheet of paper 8 × 8 inch which is first folded along the diagonals. It is also folded widthways at the point where the diagonals intersect. Then fold the whole thing double. No one who has ever built a paper airplane before will be surprised that you need to fold the top points down.

Follow the building instructions step by step so that the results are as good as possible.

Next you go on to the wing. Take a sheet of paper 8 × 12 inch and fold along the diagonals, as well as folding lengthways at the point where the diagonals cross over. Follow the standard procedure. Then fold the whole thing double. These instructions may seem rather incomplete, but the diagram should serve to make everything quite clear. Now fold the whole thing into a V shape by folding along the dotted lines.

You can't be sure of making 'The Guinness Book of Records' but there's no doubt that the Multiple is one of the longest paper airplanes that has ever flown throught space.

Now for the plane itself. Put the wing into the main part of the body and glue or staple them together. Fold the top layer of the wings up along the dotted line. These are the tips of the wings. You can repeat the wing procedure as often as you like, but don't start straightaway with a multiple consisting of ten parts. First try a triple multiple. If it will fly properly you can become more ambitious and go on extending it until you're quite satisfied with it.

Perhaps some old people will remember these, at least if they have ever been to Paris. Walking along a boulevard, through the evening gloom you would suddenly be terrified to see one of these lifesize silhouettes appearing against a wall some way off. Then when you looked round to see where the giant had suddenly appeared from, you would see a tiny stallholder holding a cardboard cut-out figure between a candle and the wall.

On his stall he would have not only pictures of famous people, but also cut-outs of monsters which could send shivers up your spine when they were projected. In fact, they were really like the negatives of photographs. The stallholder or his supplier would make them by sticking negatives onto a card and cutting out all the black parts.
If these cut-out pieces of card were then held in front of a bright lamp, the image produced on the opposite wall would be greatly enlarged. The black parts of this image were where the cardboard figure created a shadow, and the white parts were where the light shone through the cut-out parts.

If you lit a number of lamps and these were placed behind the cards in different places, there would obviously be a number of different images. In this way you could certainly create a terrifying tableau, particularly with the monster silhouettes. In France this was sometimes known as the 'Danse des Sorciers' ('Dance of the Magicians').

These dancing magicians have disappeared almost entirely from the streets of Paris. It soon became obvious that young ladies doing a striptease were much more interesting than these silhouettes, which were without any sensuality whatsoever.

It may not be particularly difficult to make this sort of figure from a technical point of view, but artistically a little talent is required. The French method of working with negatives doesn't really apply, but there's another method of making a really good phantom.

Make sure you have a bright light, a sheet of paper, a pencil with a sharp point, and some tape. Then decide on the 'victim' whom you wish to immortalize with a shadow. Seat this person on a chair about one yard away from the wall and stick the paper onto the wall with tape at the level of this person's head. Now place the bright light on the other side of this person so that a clear black shadow falls onto the paper. You can reduce or enlarge the image by moving the lamp further away or nearer to the victim. With a pencil, draw round the outline of the shadow on the paper and then cut this shape out of the paper so that you have a silhouette.

You may feel quite pleased already, but there's more to come. If you want to make a realistic phantom you must now indicate the features by drawing in where the eyes, mouth, nose etc. should be with the pencil. These are then also cut out. Don't be surprised if your first attempt is not immediately successful. For this to work really well, you'll have to experiment first. For example, try making some photocopies of photographs in magazines showing portraits of various people. If you examine them with your eyes screwed up, you'll clearly start to recognize the light and dark areas. The light areas have to be cut out, while the dark areas are left.
Once you've practised this a little, you can be confident about trying your first guinea pig on the chair in front of the wall. Who knows you might even find yourself making a living from it one day.

With these shadows you can project all sorts of interesting images onto the wall, particularly when there are a number of different sources of light.

SHADOW PLAY 2

In the past there were a number of different theatres in Europe where only galanty shows were performed. Among the most famous were *Le Chat Noir* in France and *Schwabinger Schattenbuhne* in Germany. The latter was founded in about 1910 in the artists' quarter of Munich, Schwabing, by the neo-romantic poets, of whom Alexander von Bernus was the driving force. Artists and musicians were also involved in the company.

The *Schwabinger Schattenbuhne* was situated in a garden house with a rather romantic atmosphere. This atmosphere was further emphasised by music played on a harpsichord. The scenes which were performed had a dream-like character, such as that of *Pan* in which silhouettes glided along a background of soft pastel colours. The images were accompanied by a mysterious voice reading the poems of the above-mentioned von Bernus, and all this contributed to the elevated atmosphere.

The Schwabingers also performed *Grimm's Fairytales* as well as plays based on elements of folklore. The galanty show did not exist for very long, but it did form the basis of the German shadow theatre that was revived after the First World War, because it was rediscovered not only by various youth movements, but also because various art colleges included it in their syllabus.

The great art teacher, Leo Weismantel was one of the first to describe exactly how to make these figures in his book *Schattenspielbuch*. Other shadow artists such as Margarethe Cordes and Annemarie Clochmann also wrote books describing the art of shadow theatre in great detail.

Their figures were often articulated, and sometimes the movements were even joined together. For example, if you moved the left hind leg, the left foreleg would also move. The various parts of this sort of figure would be joined together by narrow hinged pieces of wire or similar material. Thus, by pulling on one lever, various different parts of the figure would move.

The shadow artist, Hede Reidelbach, was incredibly skilled in creating these articulated movements. She made figures in which there were wires at both the front and the back, so that there was an enormous variety of movement.

In the Netherlands, the foremost exponent of shadow theatre, Frans ter Gast, preferred making shadow figures to performing with them, and became well-known throughout Europe. In his performances ter Gast used projection equipment in which the sole source of light was a bicycle lamp. This was connected to a transformer which reduced the voltage from 220 V to 9.3 V. As this sort of bulb usually only takes 6 volts, the voltage was too high and the light was therefore very bright.

Ter Gast was extraordinarily inventive, and this was apparent in the elaborate and sophisticated construction of his figures. For some theatre pieces, such as *Erik*, based on a well-known book by Godfried Bomans, he made shadow figures in which large parts were cut out, and in these he would stick thin coloured paper. These figures were placed in little windows slid into grooves, about 16 inches away from the bulb in the protector.

One example of a moveable shadow is a figure from the piece, *De Schutters* (The Riflemen) by Frans ter Gast. The illustration shows what the complete figure looked like. Even without being projected it is an admirable work of art.

The individual pieces are shown on the left page. These can be traced or copied and then transferred onto card about 0.1 inch thick. You'll see that the hinge points are formed by paper fasteners. The example on this page clearly shows where each individual part should be attached. Work very carefully and the results will be worth the effort.

The separate parts above, together form the moveable silhouette of the soldier from The Riflemen, *a shadow theatre play by Frans ter Gast. The original model for this figure is shown opposite.*

SHADOW PLAY 3

In the Netherlands games with shadows suddenly became very popular at the turn of the century. This was due, amongst other things, to the efforts of Ko Doncker from Haarlem, who had a theatre in that city which was often filled to overflowing with spectators, despite its completely delapidated interior. In those days it was absolutely *de rigeur* to have seen Doncker's shows. He was a real joker and a bohemian. He had no scruples about entertaining his rather posh audience with piquant texts and equally spicy pictures. However, Doncker's *outré* productions were acccepted without too many protestations because it was all done in such a humorous way. Doncker also made a shadow tableau for a cigar manufacturer, and this was packaged with the cigars. The cigar magnate was not over-impressed because Doncker's slogan for this tableau was 'Never start smoking too young', hardly the most felicitous slogan for a cigar manufacturer trying to make a profit.

In this tableau Johnny secretly takes a few cigars from his father's cigar box, with obvious consequences. He is as sick as a dog and makes a fool of himself in class. So he's sent off to the doctor and the doctor gets to work on him. But, alas and alack, poor little Johnny is already an addict. He can't stop smoking. This is all followed by the sad moral of the tale, which is certainly not conducive for smoking cigars:

'Little John would not stop smoking,
      What this led to, you must know,
Huffing, wheezing, puffing, croaking,
      Little John just failed to grow.'

This is a wonderful cartoon shadow story to try and copy, but obviously you can think of something else yourself. To do this you can use pictures from magazines, stick them onto card and then cut them out. Perhaps you'll become a fully fledged 'galanty' artist like Ko Doncker.

These are the reconstructed shadow figures for Ko Doncker's shadow tableau 'Never Smoke Too Young,' which were sold with cigars at the beginning of this century by way of advertisement. These figures come from the collection of Ger Boonstra.

PYRAMIDS

Folding paper ornaments is a very satisfying way of passing the time. First of all, when you're making them, and later when you decorate the room with them and a visitor makes a flattering remark about your original sculpture. However, there is a disadvantage with some of these home-made works of art: after a while their attraction begins to wear off. It's as though they lose some of their glamour and glitter, and their initial charm is no longer there. Unless, of course, you're such a wonderful artist that your work of art continues to fascinate for years.

However, as we cannot assume that you're a great artist, this is a sculpture that can be given a different face every day. It's a pyramid, which when you inspect closely, appears to consist of a number of small pyramids.
All these small pyramids can be decorated according to your own taste, and can be given a place in the 'mother pyramid' where you think they look best. The effect of this is clear. There are dozens of ways of rearranging the large pyramid to produce a different effect. The pyramid shown here is following the example of Han Makkinga.

An object that can change its face every day.

For this work of art you'll need card, glue, sellotape, a knife, a pencil, a ruler and quite a lot of patience. With these you make 19 pyramids with a square base and 16 figures described in a previous chapter as 'tetras'. The diagrams or templates for these are shown below.

Trace the templates onto the card, which should be about 0.5 mm thick. Cut out the templates and score along the fold lines. Glue the pyramids and tetras together with the glue flaps. When all these sections are ready, build the mother pyramid with them.

When making the next step, be very careful. Break the mother pyramid up piece by piece, obviously starting from the top and working down. Join all the small shapes together with sellotape one by one to make a chain. Then 'tattoo' all the small pyramids and tetras with your own design to form a decorative object which you can use as an ornament and possibly also as a beautiful puzzle.

These templates have to be cut out 19 times for the pyramids and 16 times for the tetras.

NOTHING'S IMPOSSIBLE

A popular sentiment amongst older people. In other words, never give up and don't be put off by something that looks impossible at first sight. For example, drawing a portrait of someone without taking the pencil off the paper. There are plenty of examples of this sort of thing. A sentence of many letters which can be read backwards as well as forwards. 'Able was I ere I saw Elba' is a celebrated palindrome.

This folded sculpture is no mean feat to produce. When you've folded it and shown it to someone, they'll never believe it's made from one sheet of paper, but it is. You need only follow the instructions. Just the job for an empty afternoon when the rain is lashing against the windows. The chances are that you'll surprise yourself, because it really does look very strange. How is it possible to create this object from one piece of paper?

Follow this example step by step to produce the completed model.

For this folding structure you need a thick sheet of paper 6 × 5 inch. Draw a pattern of lines on the paper as shown in the diagram below. Remember that the place where the lines end on the side is by no means arbitrary. On the long side this is one third from the corner, and for the short sides it is at one sixth from the corner, ie, in inches the lines end at 2 and 0.8 inch respectively.

The two complete lines are cut; the dotted lines are scored with the blunt edge of a utility knife along the folds which have to be made along these lines. Follow the example for the method of folding. When everything is finished, it's a good idea to put two pieces of tape at the bottom of the sculpture to ensure that everything stays in place. Now you're ready to amaze your family with this 'impossible' folding sculpture, and you can smugly tell them that nothing's impossible.

You won't believe your eyes, but it's really true.
This folding sculpture is made from a single
sheet of paper.

By exchanging pieces A and B, one of the
pencils changes colour.

A

B

MEL STOVER'S PENCIL

You'll have noticed that you're nearly at the end of the book, so what could be more appropriate than laying your tools on one side, or better still, making them disappear altogether by means of a sophisticated trick. Let's start with the pencils. Get rid of them, preferably in the way invented by Mel Stover.

Mel was a clever chap. When he invented the disappearing pencil trick as long ago as 1956, he immediately patented the idea. Whether this was a great financial success has not been documented, but, after all, for our purposes this is quite unimportant.

The only thing that concerns us is that Mel designed an amusing puzzle for which you'll need thirteen pencils of two colours, six of one colour and seven of another. The pencils should be a particular length, but now that you no longer need them, that should be easy to arrange.

What's this trick all about? With a very simple movement you can make one of these pencils disappear into thin air, and then make it return immediately in another colour. This is what reincarnation is all about. A pencil that had always been black but desperately wanted to be red. Thanks to Mel Stover's ingenuity, here's its big chance.

For this trick you'll need a piece of card 8 × 6 inch. Stick the pencils down on this sheet after sawing them exactly to size as shown in the example. You can do this with a small hacksaw or jigsaw, but it's also possible with a utility knife. When you've sawed the pencils, stick them down onto the card, which is cut exactly according to the diagram. It should not be even 0.05 inch out. Obviously the pencils should also be stuck onto the card as shown in the diagram – but you've probably already worked that out for yourself. The strange thing is that when you exchange pieces A and B, one of the pencils changes colour – strange but true.

Cut the card very accurately according to the diagram.
With a simple hacksaw and thirteen old pencils you can perform a miracle in seconds.

111

THE MAGIC PAPERCLIPS

What's the most succcessful way of telling a joke? It's always best to dress it up a bit. Don't simply drop it into the middle of a conversation, but let it go with the drift of the talk. For example, tell your hairdresser joke when the conversation is about hairdressing ('I was at the hairdresser's yesterday...' etc) and not when you're talking about politics.

When you're performing a trick the same applies. Don't just storm into the dressing room at the football club and shout: 'Look at this boys – I can do a trick!' It's best to wait quietly for the right moment and then come up with your party piece. It should be mentioned that when you do a trick, this should really be a whole performance, so don't rush throught it. The audience won't mind being taken for a ride, but this should always be done as charmingly as possible.

For example, take this trick with paperclips. It's a very simple affair really, which you can do in a couple of seconds with two paperclips, a piece of paper and a deft movement. There's nothing to it. Take a five dollar bill and fold it in the way shown below, play around with the two paperclips, mumble the magic words, and make a few hand movements until you're sure that everyone's watching, and then pull on the ends of your banknote.
Hey presto! The paperclips are suddenly joined together. How's it done? There's actually nothing to it. It's a trick that anyone can do, but obviously it won't amount to much without all the accompanying mumbo-jumbo.

How can you join the paperclips together like this, using only a five dollar bill?

SOLUTIONS

For most puzzles we describe the solution directly after the description. This is necessary for the puzzle to be satisfactorily built. For some of the puzzles (folding puzzles) we do not give a solution, because understanding the explanation will probably be more time-consuming than solving the problem for yourself. As regards the other puzzles, we include the solutions here, but before you look, have a go yourself.

The Divided Chessboard
Pages 18-19
Dudeney's solution.   Brokenshire's solution.   Gary Foshee's solution.

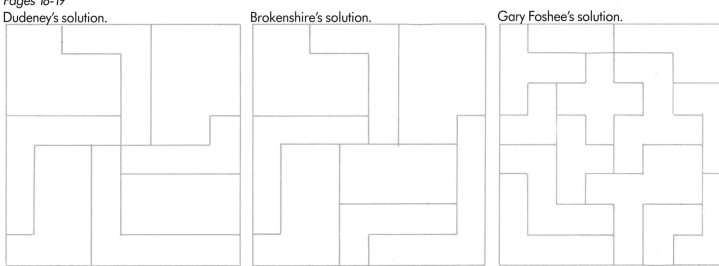

Moving House *Pages 26-27*
376437641A87659286A1
47A862957A814A9579A4
16825A86148397A6837A
60 actions.

Catching The Swan
756 v 23 v 1423 <
1423Z756143
2Z756175617424Z56442↓
3Z
7146447231
49 actions.

v   Down
<   To the Left
↰ ↱   Turn Left, Turn Right

Tangram
Pages 36-37

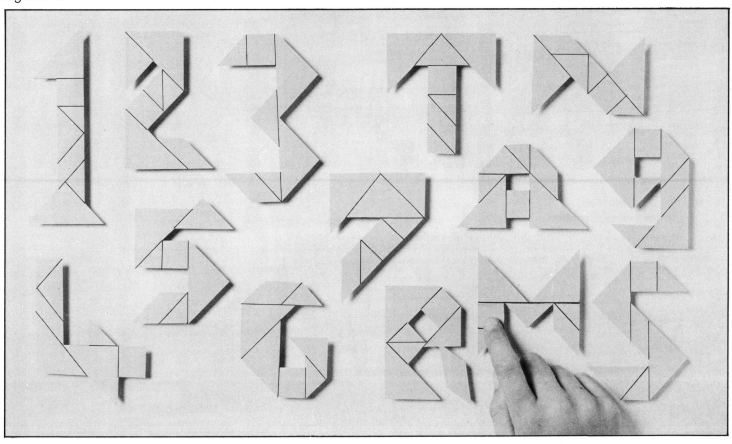

Matchboxes by Van Deventer
Pages 38-39
One of the three solutions to this puzzle.
Thank you Oskar.

Pentominos
Pages 45-47
Naturally not only these solutions apply.
For each puzzle there are at least two, to
a maximum of over one thousand.

Gambling 1
Pages 52-53
This drawing gives you the solution to this problem. The numbers indicate the result on page 53.

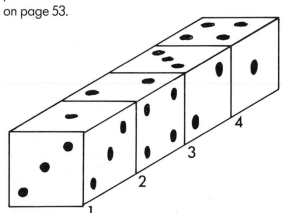

Gambling 2
Pages 84-85
And now look for the solution.
Place the following pieces so that each side of the cube shows 4 different numbers.

They made this book (from left to right):
Rob van den Dobbelsteen, Jack Botermans,
David van Dijk and Jeannet Leendertse.